AARON BURR

Controversial Politician of Early America

BY JEROME MUSHKAT

B.A., M.A., Ph. D. Syracuse University

SamHar Press

Division of Story House Corp.

Gerald Kurland, B.A., *Long Island U., M.A., Brooklyn College, Ph.D., The City U. of N.Y., Editor of Outstanding Personalities of the American Revolution*

D. Steve Rahmas, *A. B., J. D., Columbia U., General Editor*

Compiled with the assistance of the Research Staff of SamHar Press.

SamHar Press
Charlotteville, N.Y.   12036
A Division of Story House Corp.

1974

(The above card has been cataloged by the editor and may not be identical to that of Library of Congress. Library card portrayed above is 80% of original size.)

AARON BURR

Controversial Politician of Early America

The task of a historian is to use truth and dispassion in order to interpret the past. Despite such dedication, historians are limited, either consciously or unconsciously, by the assumptions and ideas of their own generation. As a result, the study of history is an ongoing process, and the judgments that historians make are often based on an imperfect scale of values that are subject to continual reinterpretations.

So is the case in American history. Yet in discussing the nature of the Revolutionary Era, historians have formed a rough consensus about that period's leading personalities that has withstood the forces of change. Among the solid "winners" of that time are such men as George Washington, Thomas Jefferson, George Clinton, and Alexander Hamilton. As for the "losers," there is general agreement that Aaron Burr is only outranked by Benedict Arnold as that era's greatest failure.

According to this consensus, Burr was a victim of his own special failings. Born to a religious heritage of deep piety and community service, he rejected both and served no one but himself. A man of intense personal charm and great native ability, he squandered his advantages in sensual lust and cheap ambition. Above all, he had the capacity to become the greatest New Yorker of the early United States. Instead, however, he plotted to destroy republicanism by usurping the presidency in 1800, and then, in 1806, he formed a traitorous scheme to create his own empire in the Southwest.

On balance, however, the historians who formed this consensus have overstated their case. What they ignore is that both as a man and as a symbol, Aaron Burr represented both the best and the worst of his gen-

3

eration. The thing that is fascinating about Burr is that he was molded by the Revolutionary Era; his career, for good or ill, was an extension of that experience.

Few men born in colonial America had a more distinguished ancestry than did Aaron Burr. On his mother's side, his great-grandfather, the Reverend Solomon Stoddard, was an influential Puritan clergyman, while his grandfather, Jonathan Edwards, was a brilliant theologian and the colonies' most gifted intellectual. The Burr family's background was equally impressive. Originally of German descent, the Burrs had moved to England during the thirteenth century. The first Burr in America was Aaron's great-grandfather, Jehue Burr, who was among the earliest settlers of Connecticut, where he became a large landowner and a prominent public official.

Aaron Burr was named after his father, the Reverend Aaron Burr. The senior Burr had been a bright, precocious child who matured into an eminent teacher and minister. After graduating from Yale College, he moved to Newark, New Jersey, where he began a Latin School for the education of young men. In 1747, he helped to found a new seminary for the training of Presbyterian ministers, the College of New Jersey, and he became its first president. (The College of New Jersey is now Princeton University.) Sarah Edwards Burr, Aaron's mother, was a religious woman, well educated for the day, and extremely devoted to her husband and family. The Burrs had two children: Sarah, born on May 3, 1754, and Aaron, on February 6, 1756.

The Burr family was destined for tragedy. Over a period of six months in 1757 and 1758, Aaron and his sister lost their father, mother, grandfather, grandmother, and great-grandfather to smallpox and other diseases. The orphaned Burr children were now shunted from family to family until Aaron's uncle, Timothy Edwards, took on the responsibility of raising the two small children.

It was within the Edwards family, amid a large brood of cousins, uncles, and aunts, that Aaron and his sister grew into adolescence. Emotionally, Timothy Edwards was not an ideal surrogate father. A cold, brusque, strict disciplinarian, he inspired respect, not love, in his young wards. Young Aaron was too rebellious to accept such discipline; twice before he was eleven years old he attempted to run away. During these early years he also developed an odd quirk that would later haunt him; perhaps in order to preserve a sense of privacy and individualism, he became secretive and inward. Rarely would he reveal what he was thinking or take others into his confidence. What began as a defense mechanism would soon harden into a harmful character trait.

In one way, however, Timothy Edwards gave his nephew something almost as important as affection. Firmly committed to the benefits of education, he hired a variety of private tutors to train Aaron. So well did Aaron respond that when he was thirteen, the College of New Jersey admitted him with advanced sophomore standing. Equally important, these private tutors helped his sister; one of them, Tappin Reeve, the founder of the Litchfield Law School, now part of Yale University, eventually married Sarah.

A bright, intense student with a thirst for learning, Burr easily mastered his college courses although he did not rank at the top of his class. But like many other students, what he learned outside of the classroom proved vital in shaping his life. He joined a literary club from which he acquired a deep interest in military affairs; as a member of a debating society he sharpened his oratorical skills; and because of his enormous capacity for independent reading and reflection he broadened his intellectual outlook. The Edwards family was quite pleased by these developments. Yet, one thing grieved them: after briefly considering the idea of becoming a minister, Burr rejected his religious heritage. Although he did not become an agnostic (he still accepted the ethics of organized religion, while rejecting its dogmas, forms, and traditions), under no circumstances would he follow the family's wishes and become a clergyman.

By early 1774, the legal profession was the only career that interested Burr. Moving to Connecticut, he began to study with his brother-in-law. However, the growing crisis between the colonies and Great Britain, which was slowly ending hopes for a negotiated settlement, interrupted his life in an unanticipated way.

Initially, Burr was not a revolutionary Whig. Just as many other uncommitted young men at this point, he was solely interested in his own career and gave little thought to questions of public policy. If anything, he was a moderate who recoiled from the prospect of a final break with Great Britain and resented the activities of some radicals who were disrupting law and order. Yet intuitively and emotionally, he had already accepted the ideology that was propelling the colonies toward independence. A firm individualist, he believed in the political philosophy of John Locke. Thomas Jefferson, too, showed his admiration for Locke's ideas in writing the Declaration of Independence; the document stressed the idea that people had certain "natural rights" which no government could take away and that these people could revolt against any government that did not serve their needs. This definition of liberty, needless to say, rejected any type of authoritarian control. As a result, once men such as Burr became convinced that the British were destroying the colonists' natural rights, they felt it was impossible to remain loyal British subjects and yet stay free. The Battles of Lexington and Concord (April 19, 1775) settled the matter. With these events it became apparent to Burr that he must fight for American freedom.

Once his decision was made, Burr immediately volunteered. Despite his youth, however, he placed a high premium on his ability, and demanded a commission. Although his friends in the Continental Congress tried to help him, General George Washington felt that the young man (he was only nineteen) did not have the necessary experience. Furthermore, Washington claimed that such commissions could be granted only by the individual states. An angry Burr resented this rebuff; it began a chain of events that so soured relations between the two that it ultimately turned into open hostility. Nevertheless, the army desperately needed troops, and in the fall of 1775, Burr gained his wish, joining Colonel Benedict Arnold's assault against Quebec City.

The wars that Burr knew about were the wars that he had read about: wars with no misery or death, only glory. The invasion of Lower Canada gave him a more realistic viewpoint. Besides being undisciplined, the Americans lacked food, clothing, tents, and even weapons. Nature was also cruel. Delayed by poor preparations, the army did not launch its campaign until late September. An early fall coupled with an equally early winter cut off supplies, sickened many men, and frustrated plans. As a further disappointment, the Canadians, rather than flocking to the American side as Arnold had anticipated, fought against the invaders.

Against these odds, young Burr exhibited such personal daring and decisiveness that he earned the respect of his commanding officers. Moreover, from a military standpoint, his innate ability to discipline and win the loyalty of unruly men marked him as a first-class leader. The same ability was later to pay important dividends in his political career.

The American invasion of Canada, however, proved a dismal failure. Despite episodes of individual bravery such as those in which Burr engaged during the attack on Quebec, the campaign was a catastrophe. In personal terms, however, Burr gained a great deal. Besides establishing a reputation for firm leadership, tact, and bravery, he had matured as a man and emerged from the campaign as a major assigned to Washington's staff in New York City.

If Burr expected his new assignment to be a reprieve from the type of troubles he had just left behind, the British forces under Sir William Howe quickly dashed his hopes. In addition to the chronic need to turn rabble into an army, Burr simply could not get along with Washington. This unfortunate clash of personalities was the fault of both men. Burr underrated Washington's ability and grew impatient when lesser men than he were promoted. For his part, Washington felt that Burr was too impetuous, and he distrusted his ambition. To the relief of both men, General Israel

Putnam accepted Burr as a member of his staff. Yet the problem was not solved; it had been merely placed in storage.

During the battles for control of New York City, Burr again performed bravely. The Americans, however, were beaten and forced to evacuate. In the retreat across New Jersey during late 1776, Burr won the admiration of his troops for his refusal to panic and for his calm in the face of disaster. Despite these admirable qualities, however, a certain petulance remained. His antagonism toward Washington reached paranoiac proportions, despite Burr's promotion to lieutenant colonel.

Meanwhile, Burr had joined a detached command that operated near Paramus, New Jersey and in Orange County, New York. It was here that he met Mrs. Theodosia Bartow Prevost, a woman ten years his senior, the mother of two small sons, and the wife of a British officer serving in the West Indies. Mrs. Prevost was not physically beautiful, but she had a depth of learning and intelligence that captivated Burr. The activities of the British Army, however, temporarily halted this growing love affair. After his brigade had fought successfully against the British near Hackensack, Burr rejoined Washington, to spend the winter at Valley Forge.

The winter of 1777-1778 was the low point of the revolutionary cause. The army, emaciated by desertions, and lack of food, clothing, and shelter, was totally unfit for battle. Luckily for the Americans, General Howe went into winter quarters. While he and his army enjoyed the hospitality of Philadelphia, Burr was not as idle. With his reputation as a disciplinarian, he busied himself in quieting restless troops and in maintaining a semblance of order in the midst of a chaotic situation.

By the spring, Burr was back in New York on a recruiting mission. Once again, his ability to attract followers through the force of his personality proved useful for the Revolutionary cause. These activities, however, were cut short by Washington's recall. Although Burr did not foresee it, that order was to play a pivotal role in his military career.

During this interlude, the British had left Philadelphia and were retracing their steps across New Jersey in order to link up with their army in New York. Washington tried to stop them: following a parallel line, he awaited the moment for an attack. That moment appeared on June 28, 1778, at Monmouth County Courthouse. What happened next is still unclear. Washington ordered General Charles Lee (Burr's close friend) who commanded the American advance, to attack. After half-heartedly following the order, Lee retreated. When Washington arrived at the battlefield, he was furious. After exchanging harsh words with Lee, Washington relieved him of command, formally charging him with disobedience, unnecessary retreat, and disrespect to his commanding officer. Meanwhile, Washington tried to rally the army; but it was too late. The British, operating under the blanket of night, moved to Sandy Hook, where transports took them to New York City.

The Battle of Monmouth was also a disaster for Burr. Through a strategic error, he had allowed the British to almost destroy his command. Then, exhausted by having been awake for two entire days, he fell into a heavy sleep and awoke with a severe case of sunstroke that sickened him for the next few months. Furthermore, the court-martial of General Lee (which suspended him from the army for one year) angered Burr and drove a further wedge between him and Washington. Burr's defense of Lee backfired in another way. George Washington was slowly gaining the aura of greatness that would almost deify him once independence was secured. In short, Burr's championship of Lee, coupled with his hostility toward Washington, made him suspect in the eyes of most Americans. This episode was to cause Burr much grief in the future.

His health shattered, Burr went on leave, spending several months in recuperation. Part of this time he spent with Mrs. Prevost. After he had partially recovered, the army reassigned him to intelligence work. During the summer of 1778, Burr spied on British shipping movements in and around New York City in order to ascertain the enemies' next move.

He performed this task so well that Washington sent him on another sensitive mission. In New York, many Loyalists had retained their allegiance to the crown, and contributed to the British valuable secret information about military movements. In an effort to reduce such activities, the legislature passed a test oath to ferret out such people who were posing as neutrals. Burr's assignment, which he accepted at the request of Governor George Clinton, was to transport such Loyalists, under a flag of truce, behind British lines. It was a disagreeable job that called for a high degree of tact. To Burr's credit, he did his work with a minimum of friction, and many Loyalists were later to be grateful for his thoughtfulness.

Although his health remained precarious, Burr rejoined the American army in Westchester County. Again, he faced the problem of undisciplined troops. However, no longer was this merely a problem of training: the men were plundering the countryside, robbing from both the Loyalists and the Patriots. To combat this thievery, Burr instituted harsh punishments, enforced discipline, and ordered whenever possible that the offenders repay what they had stolen. These efforts took a harsh toll from Burr: sleeping and eating irregularly, his health took a turn for the worse, and friends feared for his life. Under these conditions, he reluctantly resigned from the army and spent the next few months slowly regaining his strength.

Civilian life, however, presented its difficulties as well. Now twenty-three, in love with a married woman, and without a profession, Burr faced a bleak future. With characteristic determination, he attempted to solve at least one of these problems. Moving to Haverstraw, he began to study law with Thomas Smith, a former New York City attorney. As a student, Burr followed a demanding schedule that left little time for anything but his correspondence with Mrs. Prevost. In these letters, often written in French, they exchanged ideas about literature and Burr continually advised her about the proper way to educate her children.

By October of 1781, after only a few months of study, Burr petitioned the New York Supreme Court to waive its rule that a student had to study for three years before he could be eligible to become a lawyer. Armed with letters of recommendation from such influential contacts as General Philip Schuyler, he waited in Albany for a decision. His impatience became even more acute when he learned that Mrs. Prevost was now a widow and that she would marry him after a suitable mourning period. One of the friends who helped him during this trying time was Robert Yates, a justice of the Supreme Court. With Yates' help, the Court agreed to Burr's request; after a severe examination, he was licensed as a lawyer on January 19, 1782. Seven months later he married Theodosia Prevost.

The experiences of Burr and his generation as a result of the war and the winning of independence shaped their thinking in ways that would have been impossible a decade earlier. Although most Americans had not rebelled against a repressive system, the war had intensified certain tendencies that had previously existed and created entirely new ones. As a result, the entire nation was now in a state of flux. In the pre-war period, colonial New Yorkers had believed in the importance of individual fulfillment. With that in mind, they had moved in the direction of three major innovations: upward mobility in the economic and social sectors, republicanism as a form of government, and the separation of church and state. Victory confirmed the success of all three. Other changes during the war strengthened these developments. For example, the forcible--and sometimes voluntary--exile of the Loyalists had created a vacuum of social, political, and economic power that ambitious Patriots rushed to fill. In addition, the transfer of land from the crown to the states gave other men an even greater chance for success by making them independent farmers rather than tenants. Moreover, still other men had enriched themselves during the war; thus, they formed a new class in American society who were determined to use their money and position to challenge the older landed elites who had dominated New York during the colonial period. In short, the ideals of self-determination, individualism, liberty, and freedom found in the writings of John Locke and Thomas Jefferson were no longer abstractions.

On a separate but similar level, independence gave New Yorkers a unique opportunity to reshape many local institutions in light of their recent experiences. They did so in a variety of ways. The new state constitution was firmly republican, the sale of land dispersed ownership to a wider class of people, and new economic structures helped to create wider business vistas. Socially, such changes indicated that a new democratically-oriented people would never again accept the deferential colonial system which had been based on rigid class lines, governed by self-serving elites. Similar changes in attitude developed in regard to the institution of slavery. To men who had fought the war in the name of freedom and liberty, a vast contradiction existed between the ownership of human beings and the inherent right of all men to be free.

Politically, conditions had also changed. In the colonial period, two great families and their allies (the Livingstons and the De Lanceys) had dominated the state, and their jealous wrangling often formed the substance of partisanship. The war exiled the De Lanceys, who had become Loyalists; it thereby increased the stature of the Livingstons, and elevated a new group, the Clintonians, headed by Governor George Clinton. In the past, political power had rested with a small electorate, generally landowners or tenants, who were easily controlled by men of talent, wealth, birth, or close association with the royal governor. As in the social and economic realms, the war changed this political game as well; yet few men in the 1780s understood how it would be played. The electorate had expanded, new politicians vied for power, and fresh issues dominated public policy. Moreover, another ingredient entered this complex mix. Urban artisans, mechanics, poor tenants, and other new voters demanded that politicians reflect their interests. As a result, the political situation was difficult for anyone to comprehend. Some returning Loyalists fused with conservative-minded men such as John Jay, Alexander Hamilton, Philip Schuyler, and Robert R. Livingston to form one power bloc. A second group, generally comprised of men whose status had improved because of the war, centered around Governor Clinton. There was in addition a third group, much less distinct than

the others: a group which was dissatisfied with tradi-
tional politics but uncertain about what other alter-
natives they could adopt. If Burr could be said to be-
long to any of these groups, it was the latter.

In summary, then, the Revolutionary experience that
Burr's generation faced offered and demanded a great
deal for a man of intelligence, industry, and ambition.
For such men, it promised to alter normative social
patterns while it transformed materialistic opportuni-
ties; it offered a chance to be more influential in a
shorter time than ever before; and it demanded from
those who were capable of dealing with such oppor-
tunities a high degree of integrity and honesty so that
they would not spoil the system for others. Yet on the
negative side, dangers abounded. For an unscrupu-
lous, ambitious man, a man with few moral restraints,
the new society was ripe for plunder because many of
the old moral standards were gone and new ones were
only slowly evolving. Even if one were ethical, other
problems existed. Since many moral codes were in a
state of uncertainty, few guideposts existed to deter-
mine behavior. As a result, a person could be trapped
by his own self-interest; that is, what he thought to be
honest in one circumstance might prove to be dishonest
in another.

It was to be Burr's great tragedy that he mirrored
all of these values and hopes and dangers that the Revolutionary experience in America had spawned. His
failure was that in the end he could not cope with them,
and they ultimately destroyed him.

Many of these difficulties lay ahead. At the moment
for Burr and his wife, the future was one of boundless
opportunity. In 1782, he began his separate law practice
in Albany, but went to New York City when the British
Army left. It was a happy time. The older group of Loy-
alist attorneys could no longer practice and young, able
men such as Burr had almost more business than they
could handle, particularly in land claims. Almost at
once, he became one of the city's leading attorneys,
earning upwards of $10,000 a year, an enormous sum
for that period. There were several reasons for his
success. In addition to his outstanding war record, his
intelligence, his family background, and his close

friendship with influential politicians, he brought into the courtroom a logical mind, the ability to argue a point with cogency, the shrewdness to prepare his cases thoroughly, and a winning personality. To cap his happiness, his wife presented him with two daughters, Theodosia and Sally.

Yet dark clouds were gathering. Burr's wife was in poor health, and her condition seemed to grow worse because of his frequent absences when he tried cases out of town. Moreover, little Sally proved a sickly child and soon died. Aside from these problems beyond his control, Burr encountered trouble because of his own faults. By nature a spendthrift, he ran through money quickly. Burr was a person who loved gracious living: a comfortable, expensive home, good food, expensive wine. He was also an easy touch for anyone in need and often lent money with little hope of being repaid. In particular, he now began a practice that he would continue until his death: he welcomed, raised, and educated a series of young boys and girls, some orphans, some children of destitute clients, some waifs off the street. All of these activities kept him near bankruptcy because the more he made, the more he spent.

By the late 1780s, other problems haunted him. The first of these centered about his relationship with Alexander Hamilton. Since he and Hamilton were the two pre-eminent local lawyers, they often opposed each other in court. Gradually Hamilton, who was a complex man in addition to being a brilliant lawyer, began to personalize his legal battles with Burr. The two men favored different approaches as legal adversaries. Hamilton delighted in the intricacies of the law and often spoke for two or three hours in developing his case. In contrast, Burr would seize upon several points of interpretation in these arguments, demolish them in a few sentences, and rest. In these confrontations, Burr often won. The egotistical Hamilton never forgave him. On the other hand, Burr was not overly aware of this growing hatred, because Hamilton was civil to him in public, confiding his feeling only to a few friends. What began, however, as a simple difference in courtroom practice would soon harden into a deep, lasting hatred--at least as far as Hamilton was concerned.

The antagoism between Burr and Hamilton was a latent danger that would not surface for some years. Of more immediate concern for Burr, however, was his wife's precarious health. It is always dangerous to assess the mind of a person who has been long dead, but certain tendencies in Burr's life indicate particular trends. It seems clear that he sought close family stability in his marriage, the type of stability that death had denied him as a boy. In many ways, his wife had an important balancing effect on him; her intelligence, calm, and love of life kept him on an even emotional plane. When she died after a long illness in 1794, something went out of his life that proved almost irreplaceable. At this critical juncture, he transferred his needs to his daughter. Luckily, little Theodosia met the challenge. A bright, beautiful little girl, mature beyond her years, she quickly became the mistress of the Burr household. Her father, moreover, raised her in an unorthodox manner, considering the status of women in the nineteenth century: in an age when most men considered women to be inferior to them in every way, Burr insisted that his daughter was the equal of any man. Accordingly he provided her with a wide-ranging education that made her one of the most intelligent persons of her day. In addition, Theodosia displayed a sparkling wit, a lively personality, and great physical beauty. In short, she filled a great void in her father's life; the source of stability which she provided would be shaken when she left him for her own marriage.

Meantime, Burr had reluctantly launched his political career in 1784, when he was elected to the New York Assembly. A large part of his hesitancy lay in his need for money. Quite simply, his flourishing law practice paid more than did public service. Once elected, however, he gained immediate prominence because of the positions he took on several controversial bills. One of them came from the city's artisans who wanted to incorporate a closed union formed on the model of the medieval guilds. Against immense pressure, Burr objected because he felt that the corporation was basically undemocratic and its selective membership policy would in the long run harm labor's best interests. He took an equally unpopular stand on a bill designed to limit local slavery: as it stood, the bill would have only freed slave children born in the future; Burr added an amendment that called for full and immediate emancipation. Furthermore, he objected to efforts to bar former slaves from voting and tried to prevent the legislature from passing a bill to ban interracial marriages. Although he lost on all these issues, his reputation for taking a stand against popular opinion and voting according to his conscience won him many friends. As a result, a group of young men, whom his daughter called the "Tenth Legion," began to tie their interests to his career, and he slowly began to win followers among the new voters who were leaderless.

For the next five years, however, Burr's main activities centered on his law practice. He took no part in the movement to revise the Articles of Confederation, nor did he engage in the controversy surrounding the ratification of the Constitution. He did play a minor role in the 1789 gubernatorial election between Antifederalist George Clinton and Federalist Robert Yates: but he only backed Yates because of friendship.

Throughout these years, Burr remained his own man. On the basis of heritage--most of his relatives were Federalists--people assumed that Burr would be one also. Indeed, he was friendly with most of the state's leading Federalists--men such as John Jay, Schuyler, and Livingston--and his law practice, which was tied to such men, seemed another compelling reason. Yet he held back. Part of the reason stemmed from old scars he carried from his wartime relationship with President Washington, particularly over General Lee's court-martial. Another reason lay in his assumption that Alexander Hamilton, the state's chief Federalist, would not welcome a potential rival leader as his equal in party affairs. Under such conditions, therefore, Burr awaited further developments.

He could not, however, wait too long because vast changes were restructuring the political spectrum. The basic problem was that the Clintonians, who had dominated New York since 1777, were losing power because of their opposition to the Constitution. Wily Governor George Clinton, along with his equally shrewd nephew De Witt, needed new allies. Luckily, they gained an important group when the Livingstons, unhappy with their share of Federal appointments, broke with the Federalists. George Clinton also helped himself; in 1789 he selected Burr as attorney general. The move benefited both of them. For Clinton, it gave him the services of the Tenth Legion, which was growing in importance every year because of Burr's ability to attract and win the loyalty of young, ambitious men. For Burr, who was slowly becoming entranced with politics, it was a step upward.

By 1791, Aaron Burr had changed many of his personal goals. Chief among them was his decision to devote himself to politics instead of law. The move caused many far-reaching problems because it rekindled Hamilton's hostility. The difficulty began when the legislature did not reappoint Senator Philip Schuyler, Hamilton's father-in-law. Instead, by a complicated deal involving the Clintonians and the Livingstons, it selected Burr. The Federalists were furious, particularly Hamilton, even though he again confided his anger to only a few close friends. In a sense, he gained a measure of revenge the next year when he blocked a move made by upstate Federalists to nominate Burr for governor.

Yet despite these maneuverings, Burr did not feel that Hamilton's efforts were personal. Like Martin Van Buren in a later period, Burr felt that politics, honestly pursued, should not interfere with friendship.

Burr gained little public attention during his first few months in the Senate. He served on several important committes, opposed Hamilton's Bank of the United States on economic rather than political or constitutional grounds, and privately objected to the government's Indian policy because he felt that the western tribes were justified in fighting against land-hungry pioneers and speculators.

Up to mid-1792, however, Burr had still not joined any political party, choosing to remain independent. On the one hand, he was friendly with many Federalists who admired his ability and family background. Yet at the same time, he had cooperated with the Livingstons and the Clintonians, who were slowly joining forces with anti-administration groups scattered throughout the country to form a new national party, the Democratic-Republicans. Burr, preferring not to commit himself, remained a party unto himself. Despite these wishes, forces he could not control eventually made him take a stand. In 1792, he and Senator Rufus King, at the legislature's request, tried to interpret a constitutional technicality that had disrupted the gubernatorial returns between Clinton and Jay. Much against his will, Burr supported Clinton. The result of his decision robbed Burr of his independence. Reviled now by the Federalists, he now had no alternative but to join the Democratic-Republican party of Thomas Jefferson and James Madison.

Burr's critics have long echoed Hamilton's argument that this vote was an indication of his unprincipled opportunism. Yet it is not certain that these charges are fact. The early 1790s was a time of political uncertainty and many other men switched sides without undue suggestions of expediency. Furthermore, many Americans distrusted political parties in general, and felt that their presence would harm republicanism. Burr shared some of these suspicions. Once his decision was made, however, he no longer hesitated. To symbolize his choice, he and his friends labored hard but unsuccessfully for his election as vice-president in 1792. Burr's loss proved almost a victory. In three years, he had emerged from local obscurity to become one of the most prominent members of the national party. This was true at the state level as well: the Burrites, the Clintonians, and the Livingstons were now equal partners in terms of power and prestige in New York.

Burr solidified his gains during the next four years. First, he won the gratitude of Pennsylvania Senator Albert Gallatin (a Swiss-born politician with close ties to Jefferson), whom the Federalists sought to declare ineligible to serve in the Senate because of uncertainty surrounding his naturalization. Although the Federalists won by a strict party vote and removed him, Burr, who had been his chief counsel, gained enormous leverage for the future because Gallatin and his father-in-law, James Nicholson, were extremely influential in national party affairs. Second, Burr gained even more influence because of his stand concerning the French Revolution. Of all the issues in the 1790s, the one that caused the most passion was the question of America's relationship to that Revolution and the Anglo-French war it spawned. The Administration, despite Hamilton's pro-British sympathies, followed a neutrality policy. Burr and most Democratic-Republicans, however, were pro-French, both because of France's aid in the American Revolution and because they felt that the French had been inspired by the American example. Such efforts tapped a deep vein of public support and Burr correspondingly gained in stature. In 1795, he garnered more political strength. John Jay had forged a treaty with Great Britain that many Americans felt insulting. In the resultant uproar, Burr and the Democratic-Republicans made impressive gains throughout the country by whipping up a wave of Anglophobia that washed away much of Federalism's support.

By 1796, Burr was ready for another run at the vice-presidency. The task he faced might have sobered a less self-assured man. Before the Twelfth Amendment was passed in 1804, the electoral process made no distinction between the men who ran for president and vice-president. The person with the highest electoral vote won, while the next highest became vice-president. While Burr conceded that Jefferson was the party's presidential candidate, he sought to become Jefferson's running-mate, by using his family and friends in New England, along with people such as Gallatin in Pennsylvania. Many Democratic-Republicans did not take kindly to this prospect: some, like Clinton and Livingston, who also had vice-presidential ambitions, felt that Burr was presumptuous; others distrusted his late conversion to their party; while still others were suspicious of his continued friendship with Federalists. In the election, Burr gained only thirty electoral votes. The most irritating point for Burr was his poor showing in the Southern states, which some of Jefferson's friends had assured him he would carry. Ignoring the fact that the vote was less a lack of confidence in him than the result of poor party discipline and confusion, Burr concluded that the Virginians had deceived him. Such an attitude was soon to cause him more trouble.

Few things went smoothly for Burr in the next few years. In 1797, the Federalists gained control over the legislature and stripped him of his Senate seat, which was up for reappointment. Although the same year city voters sent him to the Assembly, the election proved a mixed blessing. On the positive side, he was able to give the Democratic-Republicans a vital economic weapon to neutralize the Federalist moneymen: this was accomplished by masking the incorporation of a new bank (The Bank of the Manhattan Company--now part of the Chase Manhattan) in a bill to supply the city with fresh water. On the negative side, however, he bent ethical standards when he steered a bill through the legislature that gave special favors to a land company in which he had invested. His deviousness with both bills backfired. In 1799, he was defeated for re-election, and the entire Democratic-Republican ticket lost much support.

The year 1800 marked the apex of Burr's political career, but it also paradoxically marked the first step in his eventual disgrace. In the presidential election, New York State (particularly New York City) was a key area that Jefferson had to carry. Burr was aware of the need and made the most of it. His chief advantage lay in the disorganized nature of the local political situation. As in his army career, his genius for discipline and organization, combined with his winning personality, gave him in the short run a vital edge over most of his political contemporaries. Moreover, the major elements in his political approach--the ability to attract bright, capable men who could carry out his directives, the ability of these men then to control party committees and the nomination process, and the ability to turn out the voters--made Burr a prototype of modern urban "Bosses" such as William Marcy Tweed. Yet in the long run Burr's approach had grave inherent weaknesses. Essentially a political extemporizer, he was not a team player, nor did he operate on the basis of well-defined principles. As a result, he left the impression that his only aim was self-advancement and that he was willing to use any means for that end.

In early 1800, Burr's political assets far outweighed his liabilities. At the outset of the campaign, he grasped control over the party's organization, formed a composite ticket of the party's most prominent men, and, using the multiple talents of his Tenth Legion, guided the party to victory. Since the legislature, which the Democratic-Republicans now controlled, selected presidential electors, Burr's activities were vital. At this point everyone, including the disgruntled Federalists and his envious foes within his own party, acknowledged that his genius had carried the city and state for Jefferson. Because of geographical and electoral vote considerations, Jefferson wanted to balance the ticket with a New Yorker; either Burr, Livingston, or Clinton would have suited him. By a series of equivocal moves that are still difficult to disentangle, Burr gained the nomination.

The election campaign was so bitter and strident that the Democratic-Republicans demanded strict party discipline: that is , party leaders wanted the electors to cast equal ballots for both men, assuming that Jefferson would end somehow with the highest total. In the meantime, Burr, still remembering the experience of four years earlier, bent all his efforts to maximize his own votes. When the electoral totals were counted, the Democratic-Republicans won: 73 votes for Jefferson and Burr, 64 and 63 for John Adams and Charles C. Pinckney respectively. But now the question became: Which Democratic-Republican was president-elect? Since both men had the same total, the decision by constitutional fiat lay with the House of Representatives.

People have long debated Burr's conduct in the tie election. Undoubtedly, what really happened will never be settled. One group suggest that Burr wanted the presidency and that he secretly worked with Federalist congressmen to supplant Jefferson. Another group agrees that Burr schemed for the presidency, but argued that he did not make any deals with the Federalists: rather, the argument continues, he felt the Federalists had not alternative because they hated Jefferson; thus, he could gain their votes without alienating his party. A third group feels that the Federalists, except for men such as Hamilton who worked against him, favored Burr because of his ancestry, his friendship, sectional pride, and because his election would split the Democratic-Republicans. According to his detractors', Burr knew that these men saw him as the lesser of two evils and encouraged them. Burr's defenders deny all these theories. Some of them stress that he had no pretensions for the presidency, that in fact he instructed his friends not to allow his name to be used against Jefferson. The difficulty, they suggest, was that the men Burr trusted betrayed him. Others suggest that Burr could not have dropped himself from the ticket to prove his honesty, as some of his detractors suggested, because it would have dignified the charge that he did indeed oppose Jefferson. A third group feels that Burr was so busy preparing for his beloved daughter's approaching wedding that he ignored politics and allowed untrustworthy politicians to use him. A fourth group, seeking to discredit Jefferson, argue that it was he, not Burr, who ultimately made a cynical deal with the Federalists.

Whatever the motives, Jefferson was finally selected. At first, party members absolved Burr from any hint of trickery. Jefferson and his friends, however, remembering Burr's unhappiness with them five years earlier, would have been less than human not to be suspicious. By 1802, when Burr's local enemies, particularly the Livingstons and the Clintonians, began to argue that Burr had actually conspired for the presidency, Jefferson's suspicion turned to hostility. Not only did he now fear Burr as a personal opponent, but he saw in him a potential rallying point for his enemies. Under such conditions, Jefferson began to send out signals to Burr's foes that the Administration would subtly back their efforts to destroy him.

Despite the temptation to absolve Burr from blame for his mounting troubles, he did indeed share that blame. As with so many incidents in his career, however, his activities in the period from 1801 to 1804 are still 'difficult to perceive clearly. Certain things, nonetheless, are clear. First, the Administration and the Clintonian-Livingston alliance stripped Burr of vital patronage. When that happened, many of his supporters deserted. Next, his local enemies began a bitter war of words against him through newspapers and pamphlets, seeking to prove that he and the Federalists had attempted to usurp the presidency. Finally, his opponents succeeded so well that in 1804 the national party dropped him as vice-president in favor of George Clinton.

During the same period, many of Burr's own failings hurt him. For example, although he approved of his daughter's marriage to Joseph Alston, a rich, young South Carolina plantation owner and a future governor, her move to the South disrupted the stable family life he craved. While he still welcomed and raised many young wards (such as the famous artist John Vanderlyn), none of them filled the void. For a time, until he reached a more consistant psychological level, Burr seemed indifferent to what happened to him. Financial problems compounded his emotional problems. Because of his free-spending habits, he was forced to sell his controlling shares in the Bank of the Manhattan Company, which passed into Clintonian hands. In 1803, he sought unsuccessfully, to repair the damage by having the legislature grant him a new bank charter. His failure did further damage, strengthening his opponents' argument that anyone who supported him would be ruined.

Burr's political woes reinforced all his other problems. First, because his political base was shrinking, he made some clumsy overtures to the Federalists that left them uncertain, caused confusion among his friends, and added plausibility to Clintonian-Livingston charges. Then, in 1802, he tried to suppress a book, which he considered libelous, written by one of his daughter's former tutors, that attacked former President John Adams. Burr's foes cast a different light on the subject: they claimed that his motive was simply another means to win Federalist support. To compound his troubles, one of DeWitt Clinton's paid editors, James Cheetham, wrote several hard-hitting pamphlets in which he linked Burr to everything that a proper Jeffersonian detested. Even Burr's efforts to defend himself failed. A pamphlet written by one of his supporters was more detrimental than helpful because of its attack on the immensely popular Thomas Jefferson. The newspaper that Burr financed, edited by Washington Irving's brother, could not stem the public's growing hostility. As a result, many party leaders, including friends such as Secretary of the Treasury Gallatin, remained silent and made few efforts to help.

Thus, by 1804, Burr faced a bleak future. Cut off from federal and state patronage, scorned by many of his friends, without economic influence, watched with distrust by the Federalists, and shorn of renomination, he faced two difficult choices. Either he could bow out of politics and accept his disgrace, or he could fight back by running for the governorship of New York. He chose to fight.

Burr ran surprisingly well although he lost. Through the brilliant organizational work of his friend Matthew L. Davis, he carried the city and ran well in upstate Federalist counties. If anything, the election proved that Burr was not a political has-been. Yet his strength among the Federalists proved to be his undoing. During the campaign, the Federalists did not run a candidate. Instead, they split into three groups: one pro-Burr, a second neutral, and a third, headed by Hamilton, violently anti-Burr. As in the past, Hamilton had secretly worked against Burr and reviled him in the harshest terms to prevent the Federalists from supporting him. From these tirades, a young Federalist, whom Hamilton did not know well, gathered enough material to publish a few anti-Burr letters. When the election was over, Burr lost his temper. Aware that Hamilton had opposed him in the past, Burr had always treated him with studied detachment. Now, however, he demanded a public apology. This plunged Hamilton into a dilemna: to deny his pronouncements would make him appear a hypocrite among his friends; to admit them would make a duel inevitable. Moreover, Hamilton disliked duels on principle because one of his sons had died in such a manner. Seeking to avoid conflict, he replied that he could not be responsible for what a third party reported. Burr was not satisfied; a duel was the only means to settle the issue. On July 11, 1804, the two men met at Weehawken, New Jersey. Each fired a single shot; Burr was not hit, but Hamilton was mortally wounded and died, after great agony, thirty-one hours later.

Duels had long been a part of American culture even though many Northern states considered them murder. As a result of such mixed attitudes, Burr was not prepared for the public's reaction. Convinced that he had defended his honor as a gentleman, he did not foresee that both his Democratic-Republican enemies and the Federalists would use him as a scapegoat for their own political gains. Even graver problems plagued him: New York charged him with a misdemeanor, New Jersey with murder, and his creditors took advantage of the situation to sell his house and furniture to satisfy part of his debts.

Burr's political career was now over. After serving as a lame duck vice-president at the impeachment trial of Supreme Court Judge Samuel Chase, he sought fresh means to restart his life. It was at this critical juncture that he embarked on a series of veiled maneuvers that were to forever damn him in the eyes of most of his fellow countrymen.

What Burr planned to do in the period from 1805 to 1807 is still a matter of controversy among historians. The incidents which led to his treason trial are clear enough; only their interpretation remains controversial. Some argue that he plotted treason in that he wanted to set up an empire in the Southwest through a conquest of Mexico and the encouragement of a revolt against the United States by the people of Louisiana. Other historians suggest that his aim was to mount a private army to help the Mexicans to free themselves from Spain and then assume that nation's presidency. A third group feels that his primary purpose was to start a fresh life in the West as had so many other ruined easterners before him. For proof, these historians point out his claim to 400,000 acres of land (the Bastrop Grant) in western Louisiana. A fourth group suggests the idea that Burr was a true revolutionary; in seeking to free Mexico as a Spanish colony he was acting in the spirit of the American Revolution. A fifth group advances the idea that Burr really had no purpose in mind. Rather, he promised everyone who could help him something else. With nothing to lose, he could adopt whatever scheme gained the most support.

As with so many questions about Aaron Burr, the mystery will probably never be solved. Once more, his ingrained habits of secrecy, which he had learned as a child and never outgrown, prevented him from taking anyone into his confidence and thus he left no real hint of his ultimate aims. Again, however, certain facts are clear. Before leaving Washington, he approached the British, who wanted to stunt America's westward growth, with a plan to revolutionize Louisiana for $500,000 and the use of their navy. To many Westerners who approved of dueling and lionized him (men such as Kentuckian Henry Clay or Andrew Jackson of Tennessee, Burr suggested that he would settle in their respective states. Some romantics with money (Harmen Blennerhasset of Ohio for one) were intrigued with his notion to conquer Mexico and create an empire. Further south, he tantalized General James Wilkinson, an old Revolutionary War friend and the highest ranking officer in that area, with a scheme to capture Mexico, set up a republic in Louisiana, and fuse the two with the Mississippi Territory into a separate nation. Next, Burr contacted Louisiana Creoles and filibusters who were restive under American rule. Even better, the Mother Superior of the Ursuline Convent lent him money. Another point of mystery enters here: although several of Jefferson's supporters warned him of some of

Burr's moves, the President for the moment did nothing.

In 1806, Burr and Blennerhasset organized a force in Ohio made up of about eighty men and several flat boats. They slowly began to drift down the Mississippi River toward New Orleans. What Burr had in mind was still not clear. General Wilkinson, however, panicked; secretly a paid Spanish agent, he denounced Burr to Jefferson in order to save his own skin. At once, the president issued a proclamation that warned the nation of treason and ordered Burr's arrest. Apprehended by federal marshals as he tried to escape into Spanish Florida, Burr was brought under heavy guard to Richmond, Virginia to stand trial.

The whole atmosphere that surrounded Burr was so laden with political overtones that the question of his guilt or innocence was almost lost in the larger battle being waged between Chief Justice John Marshall and President Thomas Jefferson. Marshall, in whose circuit the trial took place, had long disliked Jefferson's efforts to limit the Supreme Court's jurisdiction. Convinced that Jefferson knew of Burr's activities for some time, Marshall planned to use the episode to embarrass the Administration. At the same time, the President compromised himself. He helped the prosecuting attorney, used presidential pardons to gather tainted evidence, publicly prejudged Burr guilty, and sought to link Marshall and Burr in subtle ways so as to diminish the Court's stature. Burr was caught in the middle. Moreover, his years of frustration and disappointment had exacted a heavy toll. Still a well-dressed man with an erect military posture, his face was now creased with lines of worry. His once piercing, alert eyes were clouded; his slim, short body had lost the glow of hope. Even his self-confidence had changed; where it had once been magnetic, it now seemed arrogant and repelling.

On March 30, 1807, Marshall presided at Burr's arraignment and freed him on bond to appear before a grand jury. Then, when the grand jury met, Marshall attempted to subpoena Jefferson as a party to the case. The grand jury was unimpressed. It refused to subpoena the President and it brought two indictments against

Burr: one for treason, the second for conspiracy to invade a friendly power.

Politics did not cease when the trial began. In a highly questionable decision, Marshall all but killed the government's case when he limited the scope and definition of treason to the act of levying war or adhering to the enemies of the United States, with an added qualification that there also had to be two witnesses to such an overt act. As he phrased the options, Burr's intent to mount an expedition was not treasonable if the effort collapsed. Since Burr had not committed any such overt act, the jury acquit ed him of treason. Later, the jury also found him innocent of the second charge.

As far as the public was concerned, however, Burr was guilty as charged; he had only avoided justice through Marshall's connivance. In many ways, the justice had also harmed him. Since the jury had not decided the case on the basis of fact, Burr's side of the story remained basically untold. Moreover, Burr's silence had protected many men, such as Andrew Jackson, who might have been implicated. In the future, however, these men, who were more intent on helping themselves than in returning the favor, did nothing to aid Burr. Even many friends in his Tenth Legion now deserted him because of their fears of guilt by association. Hence, by 1808 Burr was truly a man without a country. With nothing left for him, he traveled to Europe to begin a four-year exile.

Again, it is difficult to assess Burr's state of mind. Certainly, his life was wrecked and he had no future. To add to his troubles, his beloved daughter was ill and his separation from her and his grandson was a grievous blow. It was at this point, torn from the things that he loved and from the country that had once honored him with its second highest office, that he lost control over his passions and became desperate. On the one hand, he pursued the idea which now reached almost an obsession--to revolutionize Mexico. Perhaps he saw this as his ultimate justification. When he approached the British, however, he found the government uninterested because Spain was now her ally. In the interim, Burr tried to escape his haunted past. Sponsored by one of his wife's relatives, he moved through upper-class society, where his polished manners won many friends Among the people he impressed were essayist Charles Lamb and Jeremy Bentham, Great Britain's most influential economist and moral philosopher. His social life also had a more sensual side. In the United States, Burr had gained the reputation, partially true, partially based on rumors, of being a womanizer. In Europe, he lost all restraint; in some instances he went without food and shelter in order to pay for his sexual appetites.

By early 1809, the British Foreign Office grew weary of his persistent schemes. The Spanish and American governments began to press the British to quash any effort that Burr made to find supporters by deporting him. By now penniless, his days in Great Britain numbered, Burr, in a final effort to remain, made a move that he afterwards deeply regretted: he petitioned the British Alien Office, under whose jurisdiction he lived in London, to consider him a citizen because he had been born in America when it was under British rule. Ironically, the government denied him this principle of "perpetual citizenship," which it was currently using to justify the impressment of American sailors. On April 25, he managed to avoid imprisonment by leaving for Sweden, the only European nation where he found safe passage.

On the continent, the same grim circumstances greeted the homeless wanderer—more debts, more women, more broken promises, more enemies in high places. From Sweden, he moved to Denmark, Germany, and then France. Yet through all these frustrations, Burr still pursued his quest and apologia: the separation of Mexico from Spain. He now hoped that Napolean Bonaparte, the Emperor of France, might be the ally he sought.

Burr found, however, only more humiliations. The French government proved cool to his Mexican plan; friends who had promised aid changed their minds. Even the American ambassador, an old personal enemy, hounded him. In desperation, Burr tried to spark some interest in Napoleon by suggesting a series of impractical schemes. By 1811, Burr finally realized that he had outworn his welcome. By pawning his books and some gifts for his grandson, he secured enough money for his return. Yet ill luck continued to plague him: the British captured his ship and detained him. Only after months of waiting and the selling of more books and gifts did he finally sail home.

Since he had no idea of what type of welcome awaited him, Burr traveled under an assumed name. Bad news greeted him. His sister and her son, named after him, had died; Theodosia was gravely ill and her child, whom Burr had loved deeply, was also dead; creditors in New York were ready to jail him; his legal status because of the duel was unclear; and the federal government seemed eager to indict him again for treason because of his European adventures. Yet somehow, Burr's years of humiliation had not dulled his spirit. He boldly returned to New York and announced that he would reopen his law practice.

A variety of circumstances helped him. Both the federal and state governments were too involved in the War of 1812 to bother with him. His creditors agreed to settle most of his outstanding debts. Furthermore, his notoriety helped his law practice because many people took a perverse pleasure in being represented by so scandalous a person. As a result, his practice began to flourish. Still, other people had long memories. Rebuffed by many old friends such as Henry Clay, Burr built a defense mechanism of outward calm to mask a seething inner anger.

Despite these inner turmoils, life went on. Only one thing was missing--Theodosia. In December of 1812, she boarded a ship at Charleston and Burr eagerly awaited her arrival. Theodosia never came home; her ship disappeared without a trace. For months and years afterward, a forlorn Aaron Burr made a sad pilgrimage to the dock to seek a dream that was gone forever.

Theodosia's disappearance crushed him, but Burr would not give his enemies the satisfaction of seeing him crumble. Perhaps it was such stubbornness that kept him alive. In the years ahead, Burr followed the pattern of his earlier and happier days: carelessness and lavishness with money; continuous indebtedness;

sensual activity; and the role of foster parent to many young wards. In 1833, Burr created his last scandal. On July 1, at the age of seventy-seven, he married Eliza Jumel, a shrewd, wealthy, self-centered widow with a notorious past. When she divorced him because of adultery only a few months later, New Yorkers laughed at both of them. When he died on September 14, 1836, few of his fellow Americans mourned.

In assessing Aaron Burr's career, a historian should seek a balanced view. On the positive side, Burr mirrored everything good inherent in the American Revolutionary heritage: its independence, optimism, pride of country, egalitarianism, and republicanism. Along these lines, his championship of slavery emancipation, his sympathy with the plight of the American Indians, and his advanced ideas on women's equality, marked him as one of the most enlightened people of the early nineteenth century. Moreover, as a politician he was a prototype of subsequent professional power wielders, and his method of involving the public in decision-making helped to turn the United States from a republic into a democracy. Perhaps also in another era his interest in teaching would have made him an innovative educator. On the negative side, his world had been shaken far too often. A victim of forces beyond his control, he took refuge in a life without a clear purpose. Again, the heritage of the American Revolution influenced him. Independence, liberty, and unlimited economic opportunity had made many previous behavoiral norms outmoded. In such an uncertain period where no firm rules existed, the line between honest ambition and destructive selfishness was never clear. Thus, people could never be certain if Burr's ultimate aim was to serve the people or to serve himself. It was his curse that he never made his purposes known, nor did he ever seem to live by a consistent set of principles. In short, his motives for his actions remained as muddled to the public as to himself. It was Aaron Burr's ultimate tragedy that he could not, or would not, solve that riddle.

BIBLIOGRAPHY

Manuscripts: Because of Burr's personal quirks, comparatively few of his private letters are extant. Scattered collections can be found in the Connecticut Historical Society, the Library of Congress, the New-York Historical Society, the New York Public Library, the Historical Society of Pennsylvania, the New York State Library, and Princeton University. Further information about him can be found in the letters of such contemporaries as: De Witt Clinton (Columbia University); Hamilton, Madison, Monroe, and Jefferson (the Library of Congress); Gallatin, John Lamb, Horatio Gates, and the Livingston Family Papers (New-York Historical Society); and the William Edgar, Van Ness Family Papers (New York Public Library. Some of Burr's letters and memoirs have been printed: William Bixby, *The Private Journal of Aaron Burr* (1903), Mark Van Doren, *Correspondence of Aaron Burr to his Daughter* (1929), Jean Cooke and Harold Syrett, *Interview in Weehawken* (1960), William Safford, *Blennerhasset Papers* (1864), and Matthew L. Davis, *Memoirs of Aaron Burr* (1838).

Newspapers: Burr's political and legal careers can be followed in such New York City newspapers as: *American Citizen, Daily Advertiser, Evening Post, New-York Journal and Patriotic Register, Morning Chronicle, Morning Courier and Enquirer, National Advocate,,* and the *Public Advertiser*. Other useful newspapers are: *National Intelligencer* (Washington, D.C.), the Albany *Register*, and the Albany *Arqus*.

Biographies: Matthew L. Davis' *Memoirs*, Burr's first full length biography, was written by a close friend and is unreliable in spots. Despite its age, James Parton, the *Life and Times of Aaron Burr* (1864) is still the best study written by a contemporary. The two volume work by Samuel Wandell and Mead Minnigerode, *Aaron Burr* (1927) should be used with caution. The two best modern studies are: Nathan Schachner, *Aaron Burr: A Biography* (1937), and Herbert Parmet and Marie Hecht, *Aaron Burr: Portrait of an Ambitious Man* (1967). Also interesting is Samuel Engle Burr, Jr., *Colonel Aaron Burr: The American Phoenix* (1964).

Related Topics: For a general view of Burr's career see: William Chambers, *Political Parties in a New Nation* (1963), Noble Cunningham, Jr., *The Jeffersonian Republicans* (1957) and *The Jeffersonian Republicans in Power* (1967), Jabez Hammond, *The History of Political Parties in the State of New York* (1842), Alvin Kass, *Politics in New York, 1800–1830* (1965), and Jerome Mushkat, *Tammany: The Evolution of a Political Machine, 1789–1865* (1971). Three biographies of his opponents are also useful: George Dangerfield, *Chancellor Robert R. Livingston of New York* (1965), Dorothie Bobbie, *De Witt Clinton* (1932), and Nathan Schachner, *Thomas Jefferson* (1957). For more on Hamilton use: Broadus Mitchell, *Alexander Hamilton* (1962), John C. Miller, *Alexander Hamilton: Portrait in Paradox* (1959), and Nathan Schachner, *Alexander Hamilton* (1946). For information about Burr's treason trial use: Thomas Abernathy, *The Burr Conspiracy* (1954), Francis Beirne, *Shout Treason: The Trial of Aaron Burr* (1959), Walter F. McCaleb, *New Light on Aaron Burr* (1963), and Bradley Chapin, *The American Law of Treason* (1964).

SamHar Press

Division of Story House Corp.

DATE DUE

GAYLORD

PRINTED IN U.S.A.